My First Book of
Science
Experiments

Anna Claybourne

ARCTURUS

ARCTURUS

This edition published in 2016 by Arcturus Publishing Limited
26/27 Bickels Yard, 151–153 Bermondsey Street,
London SE1 3HA

ISBN 978-1-78599-269-8
CH004929UK
Supplier: 26, Date 0716, Print run 4671

Text: Anna Claybourne
Illustrator: Caroline Romanet
Designer: Emma Randall
Editor: Joe Harris
Cover Design: Emma Randall

Printed in China

Contents

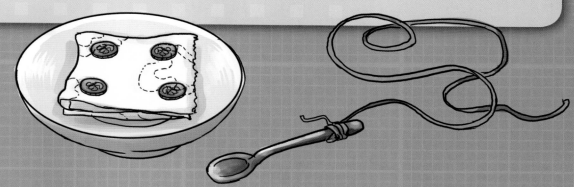

What is science?

Science means finding out about the world, and all the stuff in it. That's why scientists do experiments – to find out as much as they can! The science you learn in this book will help you understand our world.

The chapter on **forces** is about how things move. These jet planes fly by pushing gas out behind them, like the balloon rocket in this book.

Scientists studying **materials** look at the 'stuff' around us. Have you ever wondered why ice floats? It's because when water freezes, it takes up more space - so ice is lighter than water.

Before you get started

Science tips

- Clear a tidy, empty space for doing experiments in.
- Check it's OK to use the things in the 'You will need' boxes with whoever owns them!
- For messy experiments, wear old clothes, not your best outfit!
- Do messy experiments outdoors, if you can.
- Remember to clean up the mess afterwards!

GET AN ADULT ASSISTANT

For some of the experiments, you'll need to heat things, cook things, chop things up or use electrical items. For anything like this, make sure you have an adult handy to help you.

KEEPING RECORDS

Real scientists don't just do experiments — they also keep records. To do this, you could take photos of your experiments. Or draw pictures of them and write down what happened.

Try it yourself!

This book is full of easy but exciting experiments for you to try for yourself. For most of them, you only need a few basic things that you can find at home.

Are you ready? Then let's get started ... with experiments about FORCES!

Chapter 1

Forces

How do you make a tower of bricks fall over? Push it! How do you get a toboggan up a hill? Pull it! These pushes and pulls are called forces. They are everywhere, making things around us move, stop or change shape.

PUSH

A push can make something move, like when you push a scooter along with your foot. Pushes can also make things fall over, or get squashed — like when you squeeze plasticine.

PULL

A pull can make something move, like when you pull a plug out of a plughole. It can also make something stretch, like an elastic band.

Working together

There is often more than one force at work at the same time. The push of the bat makes a ball fly forwards. At the same time, gravity pulls it down.

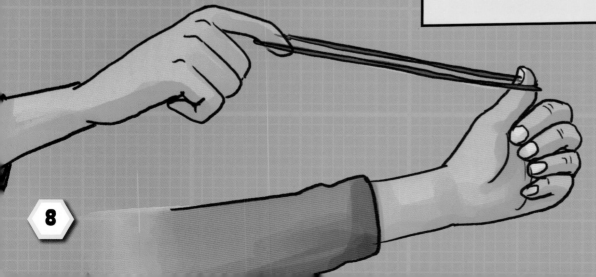

GRAVITY

Gravity is a pulling force between objects. The Earth is a huge object that has lots of gravity. So when you jump up, the Earth's gravity pulls you down again.

FRICTION

Friction is a dragging force. It makes things slow down or grip when they rub on each other. Bike brakes use friction to slow down the wheels. Trainer soles use friction to grip the ground.

Try this!

Take two toy cars and zoom them towards each other at high speed. Your hand pushes a car and makes it move.

The cars stop when they push against each other. The cars may fly up in the air, but then gravity pulls them back down.

Balloon rocket

What makes a rocket blast off into space? Rockets push gases out of their engines. The gas pushes back and this makes the rocket move. Make this model balloon rocket to see how it works.

You will need:

- A balloon
- A straw
- A long piece of thin string
- Sticky tape
- Several assistants!

1 Cut a piece of string 3-4 metres (10-13 feet) long. Thread the straw onto it.

2 Ask two people to hold the ends of the string and pull it tight. (Or you could tie it to something.)

3

Blow up the balloon. Don't knot it shut — just hold it firmly closed.

4

While you hold it, ask someone to sticky-tape the balloon to the straw, like this.

5

Move the balloon and straw along to the end of the string, with the open end of the balloon pointing back.

Try this!

Can you make the balloon move uphill along a sloping string? Or does it have to be flat?

6

Ready, steady... let go of the balloon! It should ZOOM along the string!

Another fun idea

Can you make two teams, each with their own balloon rocket, and have a race?

WHAT HAS HAPPENED?

When you let go, the air comes rushing out of the balloon. As it moves, it pushes back against the balloon. The pushing force makes the balloon move along the string. Real rockets work the same way.

Marble run

A marble can roll all the way through a maze by itself – as long as the force of gravity is pulling it. Make your own marble run and watch the marbles roll down to the end!

You will need:

- Marbles
- Several cardboard tubes from rolls of kitchen paper or toilet paper
- Scissors
- A cupboard door that you can put sticky tape on
- Tape
- Basket or box

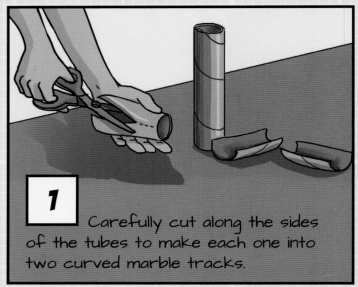

1 Carefully cut along the sides of the tubes to make each one into two curved marble tracks.

2 Start making a path for your marbles by sticky-taping the tracks to a cupboard door or fridge.

Another fun idea

Can you make a 3D, free-standing marble run? Use whole cardboard tubes as towers. See if you can link them all together.

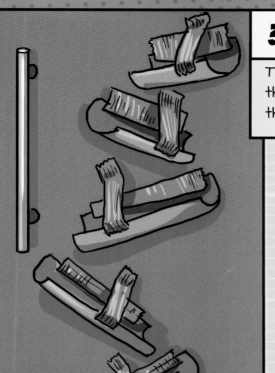

3

Tape along the side of each track, then add a bit more sticky tape over the top to make it stronger.

4

Each track must slope downhill, and lead to another track. Use as many as you can to make a path for the marbles from top to bottom. Put a basket at the bottom to collect the marbles. Now, hold a marble at the starting point and then let it roll!

5

Can you time how long your marble takes? Does it speed up as it goes?

WHAT HAS HAPPENED?

The Earth's gravity pulls down on things all the time. If there is a flat surface in the way, it stops them from falling. But if the surface is sloped, objects can get pulled down the slope, towards Earth. Balls, such as marbles, move downhill very easily, because they roll, instead of sliding.

Balancing shapes

If you spread your arms out, you can balance on one tiptoe – for a little while! Balancing depends on how gravity pulls on objects. Try balancing these shapes. You might be amazed!

You will need:

- Tracing paper
- Pens
- Card
- Scissors
- Small coins
- Sticky tape
- Thin string

BALANCING BUTTERFLY

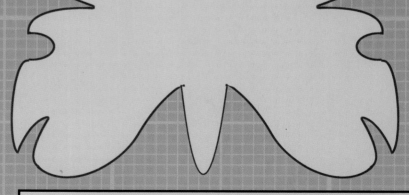

1 Trace this butterfly, cut it out and draw around it onto a piece of card.

2 Cut out your butterfly and colour it in. Tape two coins under the front wing tips in the circles shown.

3 You should now be able to balance the butterfly on your finger, by the tip of its nose.

14

TIGHTROPE CLOWN

1 Trace the clown, cut it out and draw around it onto a piece of card.

2 Decorate your clown and then cut it out. Tape two coins under her hands.

Try this!
How far can you lean to one side without falling over? Not far. The centre of gravity of a human is quite high up, somewhere in your stomach. If your feet are directly under your centre of gravity, you stay up. But if you lean sideways so that your feet aren't under it, you start to topple.

3 Make a tightrope by tying some string across a gap, or ask someone to hold the string up. See if your clown will balance upside down on her bow tie!

WHAT HAS HAPPENED?

Objects balance because they have a 'centre of gravity'. The object's weight is spread out evenly around this point. If the object rests on a point in line with its centre of gravity, it balances. You would expect these shapes to fall, but the coins move their centre of gravity, making them balance.

Spoon shooter

Have you ever tried to throw an apple core in the bin, or taken a shot at a basketball hoop? You have to get it just right!

You will need:

· A long wooden or metal spoon
· A ruler
· Elastic bands
· Balled-up pairs of socks
· Scrunched-up paper balls
· A plastic bowl

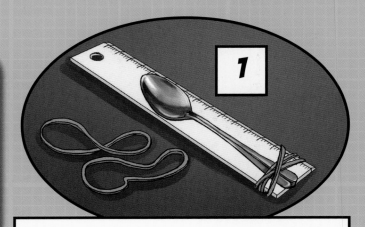

1

Lay the spoon on top of the ruler, with the ends of the ruler and the spoon handle lining up. Loop several elastic bands tightly around the handle end to hold them firmly together.

2 Stuff one or two pairs of socks between the spoon and the ruler, close to the elastic bands. This will make the curved end of the spoon stick up.

3 Put the plastic bowl a short distance away. This will be your target to shoot at. Make some scrunched-up paper cannonballs.

4

Put a cannonball in the spoon. Holding the ruler still, gently push down the bowl end of the spoon.

5

To shoot the cannonball, let the spoon go, so that it flips back up. Fire!

Another fun idea

What else will your spoon shooter shoot? Try table tennis balls, marshmallows or raisins (but you might want to avoid anything too hard or messy!).

WHAT HAS HAPPENED?

As the spoon flips back up, it pushes your cannonball into the air. Friction with the air slows the ball down. As it slows, gravity pulls it to the ground. This creates a smooth, curved path through the air. When you aim, you have to balance your pushing force with the way friction and gravity will work, to get that curve exactly right When you do – PLOP! A hole in one!

Magic magazines!

How hard can a magazine hold on? You're about to find out!

You will need:

· Two old magazines, or large, thick paperback books. The more pages, the better!

1 Put the magazines down next to each other and open them out.

2 Put the front page of one magazine over the back page of the other. Then fold down a page from the first magazine, then a page from the other, and so on.

3 Keep folding down the pages of the magazines until they are all used up. Press the magazines tightly closed.

4 Try to pull the magazines apart. Why is it so hard?!?

WHAT HAS HAPPENED?

The rough paper pages have a lot of friction – a dragging, gripping force. When they rub against each other, they grip and hold tight. You could easily pull two or four pages apart. But when all the pages are together, there's so much friction that they hold on very tightly.

Rubber slide

Friction helps things grip – but what if you don't want that? This experiment shows you how you can make less friction.

You will need:

- Several rubbers
- A smooth plastic tray or baking tray
- A box
- Some cooking oil or baby oil

1 Make a gentle slope by propping the tray up on the box. Try sliding some rubbers down it.

2 Rubbers have good friction; it's hard to make them slide. Take them off, then dribble some oil over your tray slide.

3 Now try again. Do the rubbers slide more easily?

Another fun idea
Try holding a plastic bottle full of water with dry hands, wet hands and oily hands.

WHAT HAS HAPPENED?

The rubbers and the tray grip each other as they rub together. When you add a layer of liquid oil, it flows in between them and separates them. That makes it much harder for them to grip.

Does water have skin?

Pins and needles are made of metal. Drop them in water and they'll sink. But if you are very careful, you can make them sit on the water's surface. It's as if a 'skin' holds them up!

You will need:

- Coins, pins and needles, and paper clips or small safety pins
- A large bowl of water
- Kitchen paper

ON THE WATER

1 Let the water in your bowl settle until it is still. Drop in a pin or needle, pointing downwards. What happens?

2 Now place a pin or needle flat on the surface. If it's tricky, try resting it on some paper towel. Does your pin float on the water?

THE BULGING COIN

1 Put a coin down on the tabletop.

Another fun idea
Here's a twist on the experiment with pins or needles on the opposite page. Try adding a drop of washing-up liquid to water... and the pins will sink! Soap breaks up surface tension, stopping it from working for a while.

2 Dip your finger in your bowl of water. Start dripping drops of water onto the coin.

3 Carefully add more and more drops onto the coin. What happens? How many drops can you add?

WHAT HAS HAPPENED?

Water does not actually have a skin. But water molecules – the tiny parts that make up water – have a pulling force. They pull together extra hard on the water surface. This is called surface tension. It gives water a 'skin' that objects can rest on, as you can see in the first experiment. It also pulls water together, as you can see in the second test, when the water piles up in a big bulge.

Diving bell

Before submarines and scuba gear, people could go underwater using a diving bell. They could even breathe underwater. How did it work?

You will need:

- A large bowl of water
- A glass or clear plastic beaker
- A small toy figure
- A paper tissue
- Small elastic band (or thread)
- Plasticine or sticky tack

1 Tear a small strip off the paper handkerchief. Wrap it around the toy figure like a bandage and use the elastic band or thread to hold it on.

2 Put the toy inside the glass. Use a blob of plasticine or sticky tack to stick its head to the base of the glass.

3

Turn the glass upside down, with the toy figure inside. Push the glass into the water until it touches the bottom, and hold it down.

4 Can you see what's happening inside the glass? Is it filling up with water?

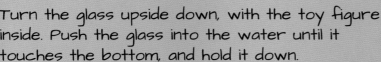

5

Keeping the glass upside down, carefully lift it out. Dry your hands and remove the toy. If it has stayed dry, the paper handkerchief will not be damp.

Try this!
Try the experiment again, but while the glass is underwater, slowly turn it the right way up. What happens?

WHAT HAS HAPPENED?

You can't see air, but it takes up space and has a pushing force, called air pressure. The air trapped inside the glass pushes down, so water cannot get in. The toy stays dry inside. If it were alive, it would be able to breathe the air for a while too. People used to go underwater in much bigger diving bells.

Fun with magnets

Magnets have a special kind of force, called magnetism. They can pull some metal objects towards them, as if by magic.

You will need:

- One or more strong magnets
- Metal paper clips
- String
- Sticky tape
- Thin card
- Colouring pens

ANTIGRAVITY PAPER CLIPS

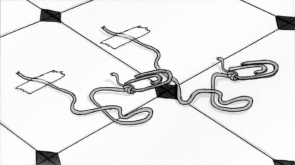

1 Tie several paper clips to short lengths of string. Tape the other ends of the strings to a table or the floor.

2 Use a magnet to get the paper clips to reach up into the air, pulling on their strings. Can you make them move?

Try this!

If you have two magnets, try letting them pull towards each other. Then turn one around, and see if you can feel the magnets pushing apart. They do this when the matching ends of the magnets are near each other.

STRING OF CLIPS

Hold a magnet up and put a paper clip close to it, so that it clings to the magnet.

Hold another paper clip near that paper clip to see if it will cling on. Add another, and another. How long can you make your string of clips?

MAGIC MAZE

1

Draw a maze on your piece of card. Then put a paper clip on top of the card, and your magnet underneath.

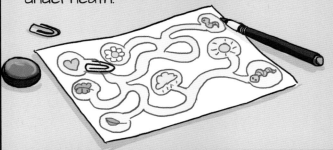

2

Can you use the magnet to make the clip move through the maze?

WHAT HAS HAPPENED?

Magnets can pull on some types of metal, and on other magnets. When a metal object, like a paper clip, is touching a magnet, it becomes a magnet too. Magnetism is invisible, and it can work across empty space and through other things, like card.

The speed of gravity

How fast does gravity pull things down?
Does it depend on how heavy they are?

You will need:

- A feather
- A coin or marble
- Two matching plastic or card containers with lids, such as sweet tubes
- Kitchen scales

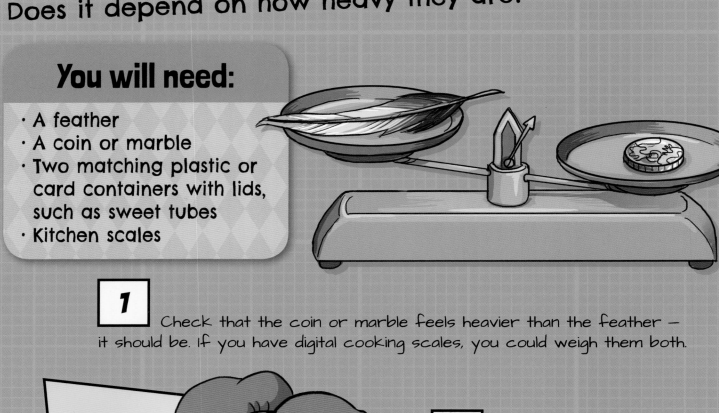

1 Check that the coin or marble feels heavier than the feather — it should be. If you have digital cooking scales, you could weigh them both.

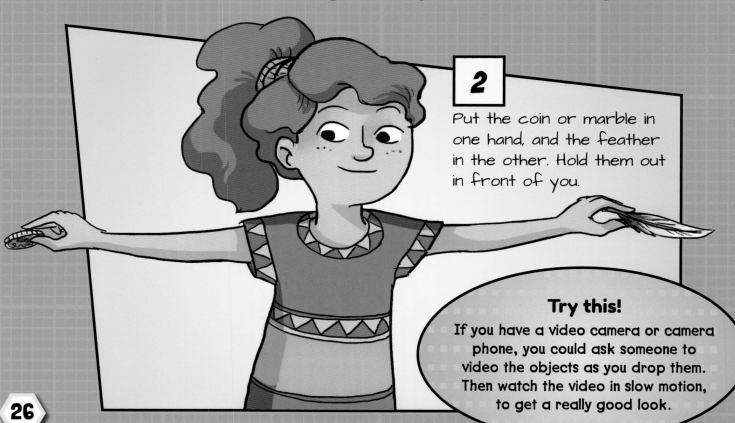

2 Put the coin or marble in one hand, and the feather in the other. Hold them out in front of you.

Try this!
If you have a video camera or camera phone, you could ask someone to video the objects as you drop them. Then watch the video in slow motion, to get a really good look.

3 Drop the coin or marble and the feather, making sure you let go of them at exactly the same time. Which hits the ground first?

4 Now put the coin or marble inside one container, and the feather inside the other. Close the lids. Check that the container with the marble inside is still heavier than the one with the feather inside.

5 Hold out both containers, and drop them at exactly the same time, as before. Now which one hits the ground first?

WHAT HAS HAPPENED?

When the objects are not inside the containers, the feather falls more slowly – but when they are, they fall at the same speed. Gravity pulls lighter and heavier objects at the same speed. However, in air, a light, fluffy object like a feather will get slowed down more by the air in its way. This is called air resistance, and is a type of force.

Bottle ball

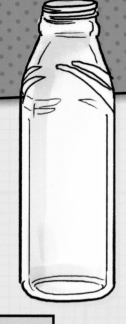

It should be easy to blow a paper ball into a bottle, right? Wrong!

You will need:

- A large, empty plastic water bottle
- A scrunched-up paper ball, smaller than the bottle neck

1 Set the bottle down flat on a table. Gently put the paper ball just inside the bottle neck.

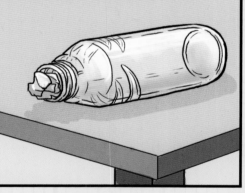

Try this!
Can you make the ball go into the bottle by sucking air out of the bottle with a straw?

2 Challenge a friend to blow the ball into the bottle — or try doing it yourself! It's impossible.

IMPOSSIBLE!

WHAT HAS HAPPENED?

The bottle has no liquid in it, but it's not empty – it's full of air. When you blow into it, you add even more air. The air pushes its way back out of the bottle, and pushes the ball out too.

Chapter 2

EXPERIMENTS WITH MATERIALS

Materials

Reach out your hand and touch something. Wherever you are, whatever you're doing, you'll be surrounded by real, 3D stuff that you can feel. There are many different types of this stuff, known as 'materials'.

Useful materials

We need materials for making things. Without them, we wouldn't have homes, clothes, books, computers or anything else. But when we use materials, we have to pick the right one for the job. The properties of each material decide what it can be used for.

Socks are made out of strong, soft fibres, like cotton or wool.

What would be a really bad thing to make socks out of?

Try this!

Find a pen and paper. Set a timer for 2 minutes. In that time, how many different materials can you find in your home or classroom (or wherever you happen to be)? Write them down.

TYPES OF MATERIALS

All the things around us, even our own bodies, are made of materials. There are thousands of types of materials. Here are just a few of them.

Some materials are found in nature, and are easy to find.

Water   Shells   Rocks   Wood

Some materials come from nature, but we have to get them out, or extract them.

Cotton
(from the
cotton plant)

Iron
(comes from some
types of rocks)

Sunflower oil
(from sunflower
seeds)

Some materials are made by humans, using the natural materials we find around us.

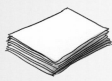  

Paper   Plastic   Paint   Concrete

PROPERTIES

Each material has its own properties — how it behaves and what it can do. For example, bamboo is strong and light. Rubber is bendy and tough.

Testing, testing!

To find out what a material's properties are, scientists have to do tests. How strong is it? How stretchy is it? Is it waterproof? Is it see-through? Try testing some materials yourself!

You will need:

- A selection of small everyday objects. Here are some ideas, but you could use other things too:
  - Coin
  - Wooden matchstick
  - Seashell
  - Cork
  - Metal paper clip
  - Plastic button
  - Rubber
  - Small piece of paper
  - Plastic sandwich bag
  - Small carrot
  - Sponge
  - Elastic band
  - Pebble
  - Modelling clay
  - Square of chocolate
  - Sock
- A washing-up bowl or bucket full of water
- A magnet

TEST 1: DOES IT FLOAT?

Try putting each object into the bowl or bucket of water, to see if it floats or not.

Tip!
These objects will endure some tough testing. So try not to use anything precious that you're not allowed to break!

In the charts

Real scientists write down what happens in their experiments. You could make a chart for each test to show your results.

Object	Floats	Does not float!
Coin		√
Matchstick	√	
Seashell		√
Cork	√	

TEST 2: BEND OR BREAK?

Can you tear, break or rip the object with your hands?

Try this!
Can you think of any other tests you could try?

TEST 3: THE MAGNET TEST

See if your magnet pulls the object towards it.

WHAT HAS HAPPENED?

Each material has its own properties, depending on what it is made of, and how it is made. For example, a thin piece of wood is easy to snap, while a coin isn't. Cork floats easily, while a seashell will sink. What would each material be good for making?

Melted crayon art

Materials can change as they heat up and cool down. This is called 'changing state'. Try this experiment to see how crayons melt and harden again – and make some art too!

You will need:

- Old coloured wax crayons
- A hairdryer (and an adult to help)
- Strong sticky tape
- A thick, stiff piece of card (white if possible)
- Newspaper

1 Tape several crayons along the top of the card, pointing downwards. Lean the card up against a wall or chair, with newspaper underneath to catch any drips.

Try this!
If you don't have a hairdryer, try leaving the card in hot sunshine.

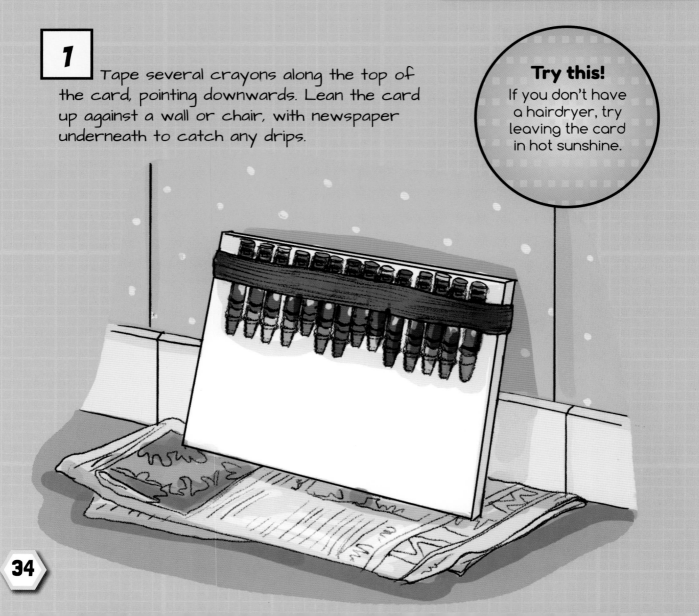

2 Switch on the hairdryer and blow hot air at the crayons for a minute or two.

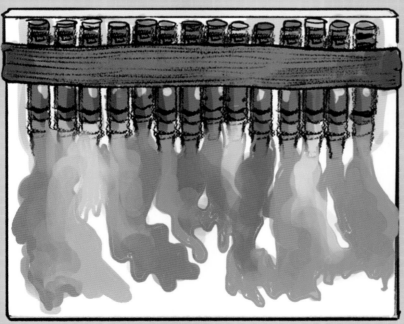

3 As the crayons start to melt and drip, tip the card to help the runny wax make patterns. Let the picture cool.

WHAT HAS HAPPENED?

As the crayons melt, they change from a solid into a liquid, and run down the card. When they cool, the wax turns solid again.

The shrinking puddle

Materials can also change from a liquid into a gas. Gases are very spread out, and can disappear into the air. Watch this happen with a puddle!

You will need:

- Some water
- A bowl
- An outdoor space
- A dry, warm, sunny day
- Chalk

1 Fill up a bowl with some water. Pour a bit onto the ground to make a puddle.

2

Draw around the puddle with the chalk.

3

Keep checking the puddle every half an hour or so. Draw around it each time.

WHAT HAS HAPPENED

As the sun and ground heat the water, it slowly turns into a gas, or 'evaporates'. The gas, called water vapour, escapes into the air. The puddle shrinks from the edges, because more heat can reach there from the surrounding ground.

The exploding bag

When some materials mix together, it leads to a 'chemical reaction'. As the materials combine, they change, and make something new. In this experiment, you can make gas fill a bag until it pops!

You will need:

- A plastic sandwich bag with an airtight seal
- Vinegar
- Bicarbonate of soda (from the baking section in a supermarket)
- Hot tap water
- Cup
- Teaspoon
- Toilet paper
- An outdoor area

1 Put about six teaspoons of bicarbonate of soda onto a piece of toilet paper. Fold up the paper around it to make a little package.

2 Outdoors, hold the bag upright. Put in about half a cupful of vinegar, and a quarter of a cupful of hot water.

Another fun idea
What happens if you mix the ingredients in a cup? (Make sure you do this outside too, or over a sink!)

3 Put the paper package inside the top of the bag. Hold it there while you seal up the opening tightly.

4 Then let the package drop into the vinegar. The vinegar and the bicarbonate of soda will begin to react.

5 Can you see bubbles of gas forming? How long does it take for the gas to fill up the bag? Don't stand too close — if you're lucky, it will pop!

WHAT HAS HAPPENED?

The bicarbonate of soda and the vinegar contain different types of materials, or chemicals. They react together to make a type of gas called carbon dioxide. The gas spreads out to fill up the bag, and pushes against it from the inside.

Turn coins green

Coins such as pennies contain the metal copper. It's normally a pinkish-brown colour – but after being used a lot, these coins turn darker and dirtier. Let's turn them green instead!

1 Half-fill the cup with white vinegar and add a teaspoon of salt. Stir until it disappears.

You will need:

- Several copper coins (the brownish-coloured ones)
- White vinegar
- Salt
- A cup
- A teaspoon
- A shallow bowl
- Kitchen paper

2 Put kitchen paper into the bottom of the bowl, and arrange the coins on top.

3 Pour the vinegar mixture over the coins so they are wet, but not totally covered.

4

Take a few of the coins out and wash them in water, then leave them to dry on kitchen paper.

5

Leave the rest of the coins in the vinegar. Add a bit more vinegar if it dries out.

6

After a few hours, compare the two groups of coins. Do they look different?

Another fun idea

Look out for bright green roofs and statues when you're out and about. They are made of copper that has reacted with the air.

WHAT HAS HAPPENED?

The salt and vinegar mixture cleans the coins, making them bright and shiny. But those that stay in the vinegar start to turn green! This is because the vinegar helps the copper to react with a gas, oxygen, in the air. This makes a new, green material called copper oxide.

Invisible ink

Write an invisible secret message that can't be seen...
then use chemical reactions to make it appear!
What will your message say?

1 Pour or squeeze your lemon juice into the bowl. Spread out your paper flat to write on.

You will need:

- Paper
- Lemon juice
- A small bowl
- A paintbrush or cotton bud
- A warm radiator or a hairdryer

2 Dip your paintbrush or cotton bud in the juice. Use it to write your secret message on the paper (it will be easier if your message is quite short!).

Try this!
Send a secret message through the post to a friend or relative, and ask them to send you one back!

3 Leave your paper somewhere cool and flat to dry. Once it's dry, you can give or send it to someone.

Another fun idea

Some other materials can also work as invisible ink. Try apple juice, lemonade or white vinegar, and see if they work as well.

4 To see the message, the other person needs to heat up the paper. They can leave it on a hot radiator for a while, or heat it with a hairdryer. Ta-da! The message is revealed!

WHAT HAS HAPPENED?

Many materials, such as lemon juice, react when they are heated. This makes them change, and sometimes change colour. The juice turns brown as it gets hotter. You can also see this happening when you cook some types of food, such as toast, cake and onions.

Make your own butter

Some materials are mixtures. They contain two or more different things mixed together. Milk and cream are like this. You can't see it, but they are made of tiny bits of fat mixed into a watery liquid. How can you get them apart?

You will need:

· A pot of double cream
· A jar or plastic container with a tight-fitting lid
· Strong arms!
· Cold water
· A bowl or butter dish

1 Leave the pot of cream out of the fridge for a while first. The experiment works best at room temperature.

2 Make sure your container or jar is clean and dry. Pour in your cream and put the lid on tightly.

3 Start shaking! Hold the container or jar firmly, and shake it up and down, up and down.

4 It takes a lot of shaking, so you might need to swap arms, or take it in turns with friends or family.

5 Eventually, you will feel the cream get thicker, then start to make a slapping sound. You'll see it has separated into a lump of butter and a runny, watery liquid called buttermilk.

6 Take the butter out, carefully rinse it in cold water, and put it in a dish. Try it spread on toast!

Another fun idea
If you save the buttermilk that's left behind, you can use it to make pancakes or soda bread. Look on the Internet or in a cookbook for a recipe.

WHAT HAS HAPPENED?

As you shake the cream, the tiny bits of fat inside it keep banging into each other. Every time they do, they stick together, making bigger and bigger lumps. Finally, they all clump into one lump, separated from the watery liquid (the buttermilk).

Make salt crystals

When you stir salt or sugar into water, it disappears! But it hasn't really gone anywhere. It has dissolved – broken down into tiny bits that are mixed into the water. Some materials can dissolve, and then form again as shapes called crystals.

You will need:

- Salt
- Hot water
- A small, heatproof measuring jug
- A teaspoon
- String
- A pencil

1 With an adult to help, half-fill the jug with very hot tap water or almost-boiling water. Stir in 10 teaspoons of salt.

2 Keep stirring until the salt disappears. Keep adding more salt and stirring, until there is a bit of salt left at the bottom that won't dissolve.

3 Tie a short piece of string to the middle of the pencil. Balance the pencil over the jug so that the string dangles down into the water.

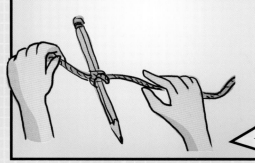

4 Now leave the jug in a safe place for a few days. Check it every day. You should see the crystals starting to grow on the string.

Another fun idea
Try adding a bit of food colouring to the water. Can you make coloured crystals?

5 When the string is covered in crystals, you can take it out and look at them closely. Can you see what shape they are?

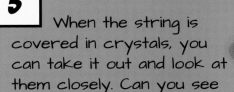

Try this!
You could look at your crystals even more closely, using a magnifying glass or microscope.

WHAT HAS HAPPENED?

The salt dissolves in the hot water and breaks down into tiny bits. But as the water cools, the bits start to clump together again. Gradually, the water evaporates (turns into a gas), leaving the salt behind. The string gives the crystals a good place to stick to, so they start forming there.

Oobleck!

Water, milk and oil are liquids. Rock, plastic and wood are solids. But oobleck is a bit different! It can behave like a solid or a liquid, depending on what you do with it.

1 Fill the measuring jug to the brim with water and pour it into the container. Fill the cup with cornflour, and carefully stir it into the water.

2 Fill the cup with cornflour again. Stir in more and more cornflour until you have a thick, gloopy mixture (you may need almost all of the second cup).

Try this!
Colour your oobleck by adding a few drops of food colouring to the water at the start.

3 Now put the container on some newspaper, and try playing with the oobleck. What happens if you stir it slowly? What happens if you try to stir it as fast as you can?

4 Try to grab a handful of oobleck, and squeeze it hard to form a ball. What happens when you let go?

5 Sink your hand into the oobleck, then try to pull it out suddenly. What if you pull it out slowly? You could try the same experiment with a toy plastic figure too.

Tip:
When you've finished, the oobleck can be washed away with warm water.

WHAT HAS HAPPENED?

Oobleck is a strange material. When it's pressed hard, the grains of cornflour lock together, and it can seem solid. When it's handled slowly, it flows and runs like a liquid. There are materials like this in nature too, such as quicksand.

Ice tower

You will need:
- A small plastic water bottle (open)
- Water
- A freezer

Many materials freeze, or set hard, as they get cooler – like the wax crayons. Normally, when they are frozen, they take up less space. But when water freezes, it gets bigger!

1 Fill the bottle right up to the top with water.

2 Put it in the freezer (make sure there is a bit of space above it).

Another fun idea
What happens if you freeze a bottle of water, and a bottle of sunflower oil, both full to the brim?

3 Leave it to freeze overnight, then take it out.

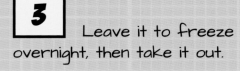

WHAT HAS HAPPENED?

As the water freezes, it grows slightly. It has nowhere to go but out of the top of the bottle. It pushes up and forms a 'tower' of ice.

Chapter 3

EXPERIMENTS WITH ENERGY

Energy

Energy is what makes things happen. When things move, heat up, make a noise or glow with light, it takes energy to make them work. Energy is everywhere – without it, nothing would happen at all!

You take in energy when you eat food, and use it to make your body move.

Round and round

Energy does not get 'used up'. It just changes from one form into another. For example, a candle contains chemical energy. When it burns, the chemical energy turns into heat and light energy.

TYPES OF ENERGY

There are many types, or 'forms', of energy. Most of them are things you experience every day. Here are some of the main forms of energy:

Heat — the hotter something is, the more energy is in it.

Light — a form of energy that we can sense with our eyes.

Sound — a form of energy that we can sense with our ears.

Movement — all movement is a form of energy.

Chemical energy — the energy stored in food and fuel.

Electricity — we use this to power machines.

Try this!
Try these everyday activities to see energy at work.

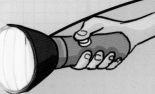

Switch on a torch. It uses electrical energy from the battery to make light glow.

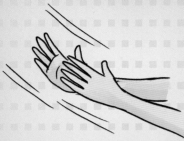

Rub your hands together fast. You put in movement energy, and your hands warm up.

Hit a pan with a wooden spoon. You put in movement energy, using your arm. It turns into sound energy.

Heat is movement

When things are hot, it actually means they are moving more. These experiments will show you how!

You will need:

- Hot tap water (not too hot to touch)
- Cold water
- Two glasses
- Three bowls
- Food colouring
- Two hands

COOL COLOURS

1 Half-fill one glass with hot tap water, and the other with cold water. Stand them side by side.

Another fun idea
Instead of food colouring, try mixing in sugar. Does it dissolve faster in hot water, or cold?

2 Drop one drop of food colouring into each glass. Watch them closely. What happens?

HOT AND COLD

1 Now half-fill one bowl with hot water, and another with cold water. Stand them side by side.

2 In the third bowl, mix equal amounts of hot and cold water to make lukewarm water.

3 Put one hand in the hot water and the other in the cold water, and leave them there for one minute.

4 Now take both your hands out, and put them together into the bowl of lukewarm water. How does it feel?

WHAT HAS HAPPENED?

The food colouring spreads out faster in the hot water than in the cold water. That's because when the water is warmer, its molecules (the tiny parts it is made of) contain more movement energy. They move faster, and push the food colouring around.

Colder

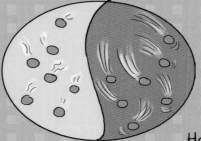

Hotter

Hot and cold hands

When warmer and colder things meet, the movement of the warmer things pushes against the colder things, and warms them up. Your hands aren't very good at sensing temperature. Instead, they sense whether they are losing heat energy, or getting more. The cold hand is getting more heat energy, so it feels warm. The warm hand is losing heat energy, so it feels cold.

Getting bigger

When things get hotter, the molecules in them move faster. That makes them push away from each other, and they take up more space.

You will need:

- A bag of marshmallows
- A microwaveable plate
- A microwave oven
- A glass bottle
- A coin that covers the opening of the bottle
- A sink with hot and cold taps

THE MIGHTY MARSHMALLOW

1 First, microwave your marshmallow. Put one marshmallow on the plate, and put it in the microwave.

2 Switch the microwave on, on normal power, for 10-15 seconds. Open the door as soon as it stops.

3 Compare the marshmallow with another one from the bag. What's the difference?

Watch out!
The marshmallow could be very hot at first. You can eat it, but wait for it to cool for a minute before you do!

56

BOTTLE BLAST

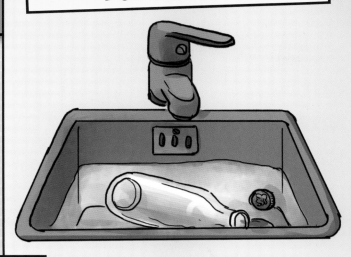

1   Run cold water into the sink. Put the glass bottle and the coin in to get nice and cold. Then take out the bottle and drain the water from the sink.

2   Empty the bottle and stand it up. Put the wet coin over the top of it.

3   Run hot water into the sink to make a shallow bath, and stand the bottle in it. What happens?

Another fun idea
What happens if you put a balloon over the neck of the bottle?

WHAT HAS HAPPENED?

Marshmallows contain lots of tiny air bubbles. As they heat up, the molecules in the air move faster, and push against each other. The air bubbles get bigger, making the marshmallow grow. The same thing happens inside the bottle. The air warms up and gets bigger. It pushes at the coin on top of the bottle, making it jump.

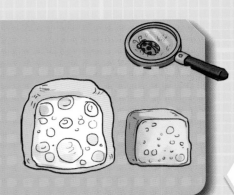

Magic marbles

The energy of a moving marble can behave in a strange way!

You will need:

· A medium-sized piece of card
· Five marbles or marble-sized balls

1 Fold the card in half down the middle, then make two more folds the other way to make a channel, like this.

2 Put your marbles in a row in the channel, like this. They should all be touching each other.

3 Roll one marble back away from the others, then flick it gently towards them. What do you think will happen?

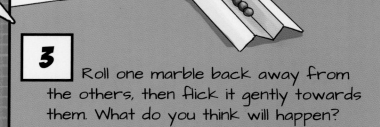

WHAT HAS HAPPENED?

When the moving marble hits the others, they don't all move! Only the one on the other end does. As the first marble hits the second, it passes movement energy into it. The second hits the third, the third hits the fourth, and so on, all passing their energy on. Only the last marble moves, because it has space to.

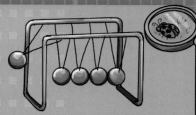

This toy, called Newton's cradle, works the same way.

Sound is movement

How can you make a balloon buzz?
Try this experiment.

1 Put the coin or nut inside the balloon. Blow up the balloon until it's quite big, then tie it closed.

You will need:

- A balloon
- A coin with lots of sides, or a hexagonal nut

2 Hold the balloon by the top and move it around in a circle, to make the coin or nut whirl around inside. Can you hear a buzz?

Watch out!
Keep the coin or nut in the bottom of the balloon, away from your mouth, as you blow.

Another fun idea
Put your hands around the balloon, and hold it up to a working radio speaker. You'll feel it vibrating!

WHAT HAS HAPPENED?

Sound is a form of energy that is made when objects vibrate, or move quickly to and fro. As the coin or nut whirls around, its corners bump against the balloon, making it vibrate very quickly. This makes a high buzzing sound!

Sound in a spoon!

In this experiment, you can find out how the same noise can sound very different, depending on how it travels.

You will need:

- String
- Scissors
- Two metal spoons

1 Cut a piece of string about as long as your arm. Tie one end around the handle of one of the spoons.

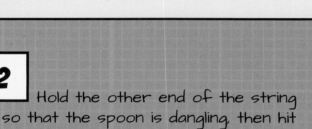

2 Hold the other end of the string so that the spoon is dangling, then hit the spoon with the other spoon.

3 What kind of noise does it make? Is it easy to hear? What does it remind you of?

4

Now wrap the end of the string around the tip of your finger, and press your finger against your ear.

Watch out!
Don't stick your finger right inside your ear, as this can be bad for it. Just press it against your ear.

5

Hit the spoon again. Does it sound different? What is different about it?

Another fun idea
Try tying two or more spoons to a longer piece of string. Hold both ends to your ears – or have two people listen to one end each!

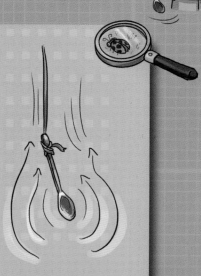

WHAT HAS HAPPENED?

Our ears hear sounds because the vibrations that make the sound spread out through the air. The spoon vibrates, it makes the air vibrate, and the vibrations (called sound waves) hit your ears.

But when you press the string against your ear, the sound vibrations spread to your ear along the string, and through your finger and your head. Sound waves travel much faster and better through solid things than they do through air. So this way, the spoon noise sounds louder and stronger.

See a sound before you hear it

Sound takes time to travel through the air. Light moves much more quickly than sound, and that means you can sometimes see someone making a noise before you hear anything!

1 First, measure out a big distance on the ground — 200 metres (or 200 yards) is perfect. If it's too hard to measure, just take big steps and count the number of steps.

29...30!

You will need:

- A friend or family member to help
- Two old pans or other noisy metal objects, such as buckets
- A very big open space
- A stopwatch or smartphone timer
- A tape measure (optional)

2 One person stands at one end with the two pans. The other stands at the other end with the stopwatch, ready to start it. You must be able to see each other!

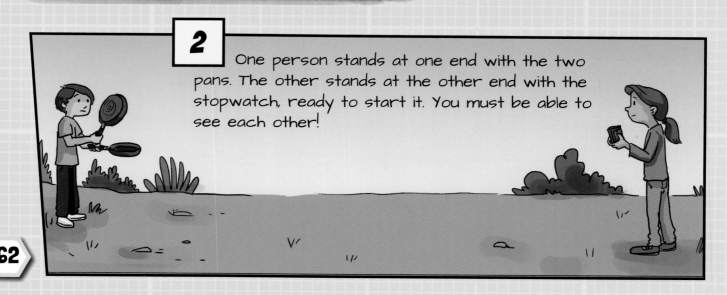

3 The person with the pans should hold them wide apart, then bash them together. At the moment they see the pans touch, the other person should start the stopwatch.

Try this!

Can you use maths to work out how fast the sound was moving?

WHAT HAS HAPPENED?

When something makes a sound, the sound vibrations spread out through the air. This means you don't hear sounds straight away – it takes a little while for them to travel to you. When you are close to things, it happens quickly and you don't notice it. But when you are far away, you can see something noisy happening, but not hear it until a little while later.

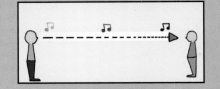

4 The person with the stopwatch should stop it as soon as they hear the crash of the pans being banged together. How long did the sound take to reach them?

Make a rainbow

Light usually looks white or yellowish. But it is actually made up of all the colours of the rainbow. Here's how to see them.

1

Place the container in bright, direct sunlight (either outdoors, or by a window where the Sun is shining in).

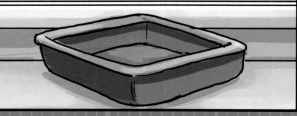

You will need:

- A bright, sunny day
- A small mirror (that you can get wet)
- A piece of white paper or card
- A shallow plastic container
- Water

2

Pour water into the container until it is as deep as the size of the mirror. Put the mirror into the water.

3

Position the mirror so that the Sun shines onto it. Position the white card to catch the light reflected from the mirror.

4 Gently tilt and move the mirror to get the best position. You should see a pattern of rainbow colours on the card.

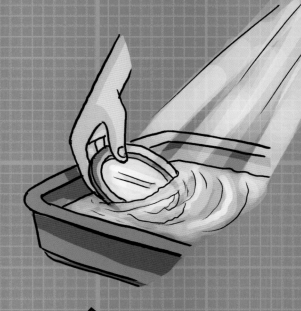

Another fun idea

You can also make a rainbow using a garden hose on a sunny day. Stand with your back to the Sun, and spray a fine mist of water. You should see a rainbow appear in the mist.

WHAT HAS HAPPENED?

White light, like the light that shines from the Sun, is made up of a range, or spectrum, of different colours. When light passes in and out of different see-through substances, such as water and air, it bends, or refracts. The different colours of light bend different amounts. This makes them separate out from each other, and appear as a rainbow of colours.

Scientists use a shaped piece of glass called a prism to split light into its colours.

Make a periscope

Light reflects, or bounces, off mirrors. You can use this to help you look around a corner, by making a periscope!

You will need:

- A long cardboard box or container, such as a cling film or food bag box
- Two small mirrors that will fit inside the box
- Plasticine or sticky tack
- Marker pen
- Scissors

1 Open the side of the box so that you can see what you are doing. Some boxes will have a lid that opens, like this.

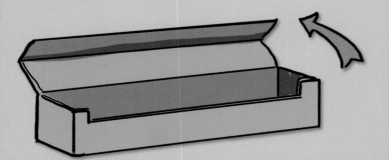

2 Mark two windows on the box — one at one end of a long side, and one at the other end on the opposite side. Carefully cut them out.

3 Put a large blob of plasticine or sticky tack inside the corner opposite each window. Press the blobs into the corners.

4 Press the two mirrors onto the blobs so that they are positioned diagonally opposite the windows.

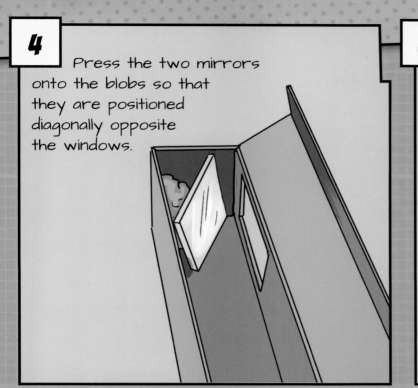

5 You should now be able to look into one window, and see out of the other. If you can't, adjust the angles of the mirrors until it works.

6 Close the side of the box. Your periscope is now ready! You can use it to look around a corner or over a wall.

WHAT HAS HAPPENED?

Light travels in straight lines. When it hits a mirror, it bounces off. If the mirror is flat, the light will bounce back the way it came. But if the mirror is at an angle, the light will bounce off in a different direction. The angled mirrors make light coming in at one window bounce along the tube, and travel out of the other window.

Sparks in the dark

Light shines from the Sun and stars, lamps, candles and screens. But there's another, very strange kind of light that can come from things being crushed or ripped.

1 First, set up a dark place. It could be a room with a blackout blind, a dark garden at night, or you could make a dark den under a large duvet.

2 Prepare your experiments with the light on, before taking them into the dark to try out. Wait in the dark for a few minutes before you start, to help your eyes see the sparks better.

TEST 1:

Preparation:

1. Put some sugar lumps in the sandwich bag. Seal it closed.
2. Stick two strips of tape together, with the ends apart and folded over.
3. Seal the envelope closed.

Using the pliers, crush the sugar lumps through the bag, and look for flashes of light as they break apart. (Don't nip your fingers! You might want to get an adult to do this job.)

TEST 2:

Take your sealed self-seal envelope and pull open the seal. You may see sparks of light where the glue comes apart.

TEST 3:

Hold the two folded ends of the tape and rip them apart. Can you see light glowing? Sometimes, pulling tape from the roll can also make light.

WHAT HAS HAPPENED?

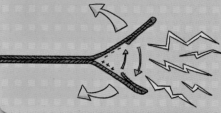

This kind of light has a long name – triboluminescence (say try-boe-loo-min-ess-ens). It happens when some types of chemicals break apart.

Static electric games

Electricity is a form of energy. One type of electricity is called static. It can build up in objects, and make them behave in weird ways.

TO BEGIN...

Rub the balloon several times on the woolly surface. Only rub in one direction, then lift the balloon and rub again.

You will need:

- Balloons
- A woolly jumper, blanket or scarf
- A wall
- Tissue paper
- Empty drinks cans

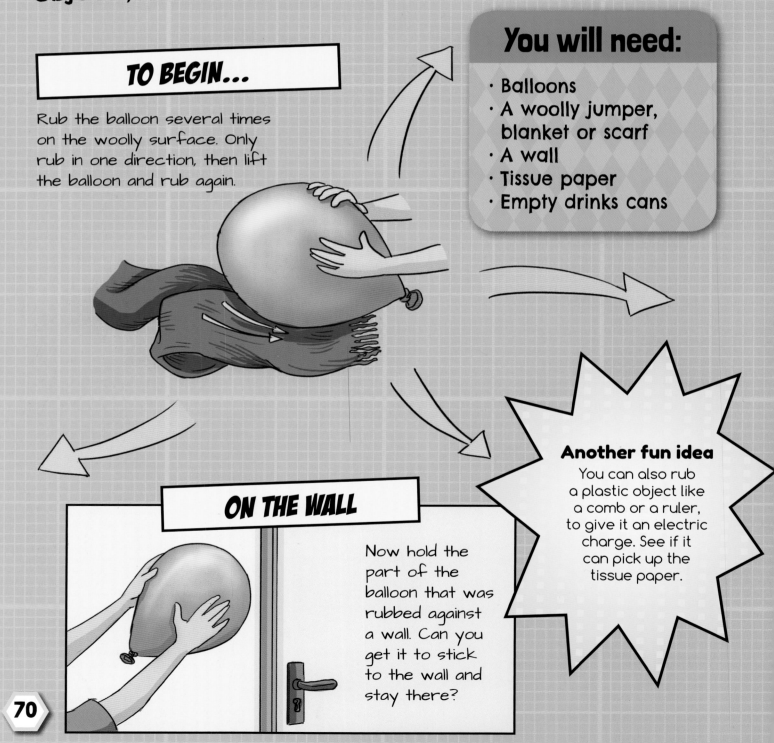

Another fun idea

You can also rub a plastic object like a comb or a ruler, to give it an electric charge. See if it can pick up the tissue paper.

ON THE WALL

Now hold the part of the balloon that was rubbed against a wall. Can you get it to stick to the wall and stay there?

HAIR-RAISING

Rub the balloon on your hair. Then slowly lift the balloon up... and it should pull your hair up with it!

Tear some tissue paper into tiny pieces. Rub the balloon on the wool again, then hold it over the tissue paper. Does it pull them up like a magnet?

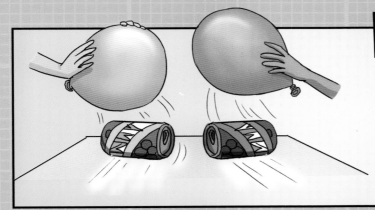

CAN RACE

For this experiment, you need two people. Place two empty drinks cans on their sides. Rub two balloons on the scarf. Hold the balloons near the cans, and they will start to roll. Who can make theirs go fastest?

WHAT HAS HAPPENED?

Objects contain tiny bits called electrons, which can move. Moving electrons make electricity. When you rub the balloon on the wool, some electrons move from the wool into the balloon. This makes an electrical pull, or charge, between the balloon and other objects.

The broken straw

How can a straw be whole, but look as if it's in two pieces? All you need is water.

You will need:
- A glass
- A straw
- Water

1 Fill the glass with water almost to the top.

2 Put the straw into the water so that it leans over sideways.

Did you know?
Objects like straws don't shine with light. But you see them because light from the Sun, or a lamp, bounces off them and enters your eyes.

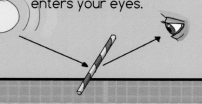

3 Look at the straw from the side. What has happened to it?

WHAT HAS HAPPENED?

The straw is just the same as it always was, but it looks different. This is because of refraction – the way light bends when it passes in or out of something see-through. Part of the straw is in the air, and the light from it comes straight to your eyes. Part of it is in the water, and the light from it bends as it moves through water and glass on its way to you. So the two parts look as if they are in different places.

Chapter 4

EXPERIMENTS WITH LIVING THINGS

Living things

What makes you different from a coin, a spoon or a lump of ice? You're alive – an eating, breathing, growing, living thing. Our world is full of living things, from humans like you to huge whales, trees and flowers, dogs and cats, insects and tiny germs.

What are living things?

There are millions of types of living things, and they are all different. But there are some things that all living things do...

THEY MOVE...

Plants lean towards the Sun.

People walk, run or dance.

THEY FEED...

Lions eat antelopes.

This toadstool feeds on a rotting tree stump.

THEY SENSE...

Plants sense light.

A shark sniffs out its prey.

You grow as you get older.

A sunflower grows very tall.

THEY MAKE MORE LIVING THINGS!

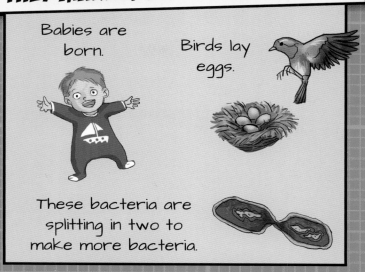

Babies are born.

Birds lay eggs.

These bacteria are splitting in two to make more bacteria.

Which is which?

The types of living things are called species. Each species is different and has its own name. The species can be divided into larger groups.

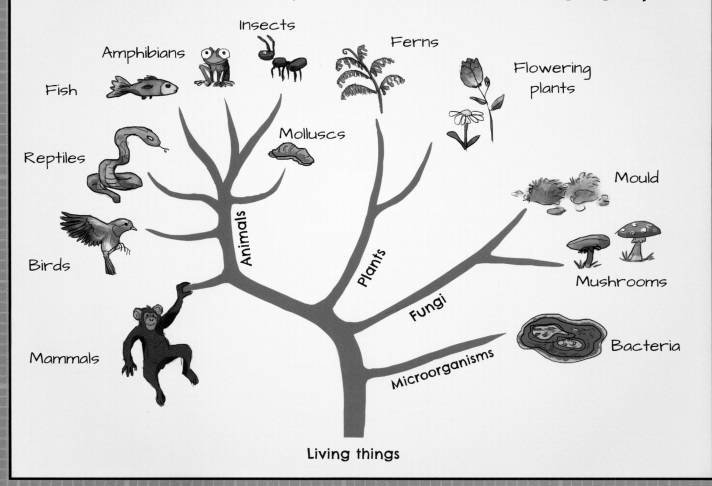

Insects

Amphibians

Ferns

Fish

Flowering plants

Reptiles

Molluscs

Mould

Birds

Animals

Plants

Mushrooms

Fungi

Mammals

Bacteria

Microorganisms

Living things

Grass caterpillar

Create your own caterpillar, and watch it grow grassy hair! This experiment lets you see how plants grow.

1 Mix a handful of grass seeds with several handfuls of compost. Cut off one leg of the tights, and pour the mixture in.

2 Tie the leg closed at the open end. Snip it off neatly. Stretch three or four elastic bands around the caterpillar to divide it into sections and a head.

3 Stick some googly eyes on the head (or make your own using buttons or card). Put the caterpillar on a tray or plate.

4 Put the tray or plate with your caterpillar on it, on a sunny windowsill. If it's spring or summer, it could go outside in a garden or on a balcony.

5 Water your caterpillar's body every day, making sure it stays damp. Soon, its hair will start to appear! How long does it take to grow?

Another fun idea

What happens if you make a caterpillar, but leave it somewhere dark? What happens if you don't water it? Try these tests to see what conditions seeds need to grow properly.

WHAT HAS HAPPENED?

When the grass seeds have plenty of light, water and soil, they start to grow. They grow roots and long leaves, which look like furry hair.

Rainbow celery

Have you ever seen a plant with red or blue leaves? Here's a clever way to make a stick of celery change colour. It will look like magic!

You will need:

- Sticks of celery with leaves
- Two small glasses
- Red and blue food colouring
- Water
- Kitchen scissors

1

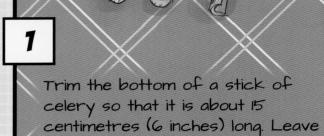

Trim the bottom of a stick of celery so that it is about 15 centimetres (6 inches) long. Leave the leaves on.

2

Pour water into a glass so it is a third full. Add a small amount of food colouring.

3 Put the end of the celery into the liquid in the glass. Leave the glass in a safe place, where it won't be moved.

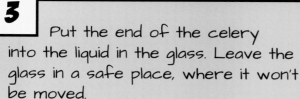

4 After one day, cut across the base of the celery with scissors. You will see lines of colour rising up the stalk.

5 Put water and a small amount of food colouring in two glasses. Split another stick of celery. Allow each part of the split stalk to stand in a glass.

6 On the following day, you will have multi-coloured celery! Cut back the stalks to check.

WHAT HAS HAPPENED?

Plants need water, just like we do. They take up water through their roots. The water travels in little tubes, all the way through the stem to the leaves. If you put dye in the water, the coloured water will be carried to the leaves too!

Another fun idea
Put a flower with white petals in water with food colouring. Leave it overnight. What do you think will happen?

Dried fruit

There's one thing that all living things need, and that's water. In this experiment, you can find out just how watery plants are.

You will need:

- A selection of fruit, such as an orange, an apple, a peach and a banana
- A knife
- An oven
- A baking tray
- Weighing scales
- Pencil and paper
- An adult to help

1

Weigh each fruit, and write down how much it weighs. Then slice up each fruit thinly. Spread the slices out on the baking tray.

2 With an adult's help, put the tray in the oven. Set it to the lowest heat — usually about 100°C (225°F or gas mark ¼). Leave it for about 6 hours, or overnight.

3

Carefully take out the tray of dried-out fruit. Leave it to cool. Once cool, weigh each fruit again. How much less does each weigh?

WHAT HAS HAPPENED?

Living things are made of tiny units called cells. Cells need water to make them work. Plants also take in water in order to make food and grow. A typical fruit is over 80% (or fourth-fifths) water. A human is a bit less watery – around 60-70%.

Flower photos

You will need:

- A flower, such as a rose, poppy, carnation or daffodil, that is just starting to open (from your garden or a flower shop)
- A vase or jug of water
- A digital or smartphone camera
- A tripod, or some plasticine or sticky tack.
- A brightly lit room
- A computer

Take a series of flower photos to see how a flower opens its petals and blooms. You'll need to start in the morning – it could take the whole day!

1 Stand your flower in the vase or jug of water. Set up your camera pointing at the flower. If you don't have a tripod, use plasticine or sticky tack to hold it still.

2 Take a photo of the flower every 20 or 30 minutes. Make sure you keep the lights on all day so it is easy to see.

3 Once the flower has opened, upload all your photos onto a computer. Arrange them in order of the time they were taken.

WHAT HAS HAPPENED?

It's hard to see a flower opening, as it moves so slowly. But your photos let you see how it happens.

The rubbery bone

Bones are hard – aren't they? They hold your body up, and protect soft parts, like your brain. But you can make a bone go bendy and rubbery. Here's how!

You will need:

- A cooked chicken bone
- A plastic food container with a lid
- White vinegar
- Kitchen paper

1 First, you'll need to get your bone. The best way is to pull apart a well-cooked chicken leg. Take the bone out, and wash it well.

Try this!
Can you feel some of the hard bones in your body? Try feeling your head, cheeks, ankles and knees.

2 Put the bone in the container, then pour in enough white vinegar to cover it completely. Put the lid on tightly.

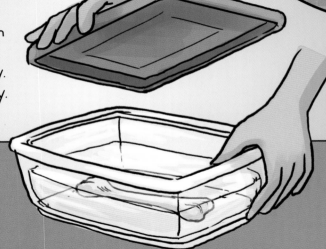

3

Leave the container somewhere safe for at least five days. Then open it, take the bone out, wash it and dry it with kitchen paper.

4

You'll find the bone has become rubbery and soft! Can you bend it in half? Can you tie a knot in it?

Did you know?

Dairy foods like milk and cheese contain calcium. That's why they are good for helping your body to grow strong bones and teeth. If you can't eat dairy foods, though, you can also get calcium from leafy vegetables like cabbage, beans, sardines, oranges and nuts.

WHAT HAS HAPPENED?

Animal bones – including your own – contain a mineral called calcium. It is what makes bones hard and strong. Vinegar is good at dissolving calcium. When it soaks into the bone, the calcium dissolves away. The softer, bendy parts of the bone are left behind.

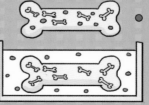

● = calcium

Bone soaking in vinegar

Fly-eye glasses

Lots of animals have eyes. They use them to sense light, which helps them to tell where objects are. But not all eyes are the same. Make these glasses, and see the world through a fly's eyes!

You will need:

· Card
· Marker pen
· Scissors
· Bubble wrap
· Glue or sticky tape

1 Draw a pair of large round glasses onto the card, like this. Include the arms of the glasses sticking out at the sides.

2 Carefully cut out your glasses, including the holes for the eyes. Fold the arms inwards, then check that your glasses fit you.

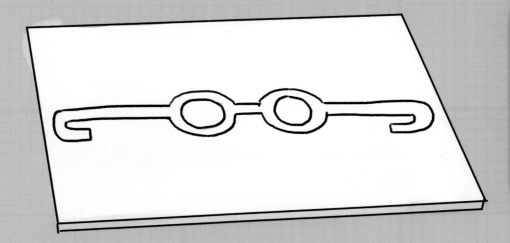

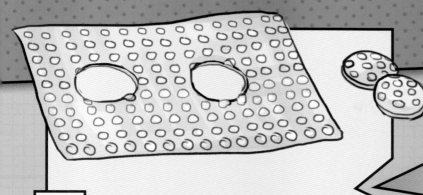

3

On your bubble wrap, draw two circles, the same size as the frames of your glasses. Cut them out.

Another fun idea

With the glasses off, try covering one eye and looking around. Do things look different? Your two eyes give you two slightly different views of the world. This lets you see in 3D, and judge how far away things are.

4

Glue or sticky tape the bubble wrap circles to the inside of your glasses frames. Once they are firmly in place, try out your glasses!

WHAT HAS HAPPENED?

Flies and many other insects have special eyes called compound eyes. They are made up of lots of mini eyes, all tightly packed together. The fly sees an image of the world divided into small sections – like looking through bubble wrap.

Try this!

If you can catch a fly in a glass, try looking at it closely. You could use a magnifying glass, if you have one. Can you see its compound eyes?

Growing dough

Cut a slice of bread, and you'll see it's full of bubbles. But did you know what makes those bubbles? The answer is: tiny living things.

You will need:

- 500 grams (about 1 pound) of bread flour
- 1 sachet of dried yeast
- 1 teaspoon of salt
- 1 teaspoon of sugar
- Olive oil
- 300ml (10 fluid ounces) of warm water
- A mixing bowl
- Cling film
- A baking tray
- An adult to help

1
Put the flour, yeast and salt in the bowl. Mix the sugar and 1 tablespoon of oil into the water, then add the water to the flour. Use your hands to mix it together.

2
Shape and squeeze the mixture to make a soft dough. Tip it out onto a table sprinkled with flour, and knead it for 5 minutes.

Tip!
Here's how to knead:
Fold the dough in half.
Press it down with both hands.
Stretch it out a bit sideways.
Fold in half again... and carry on!

3
Oil the baking tray. Put your dough on it. Oil the top of the dough, then spread a piece of cling film over it. Leave the dough in a warm place for an hour.

Another fun idea
You can make bread dough into shapes before leaving them to rise. (They will need less cooking time – about 10 minutes.)

4 After an hour, the dough should be much bigger! Now get ready to bake it in the oven to make bread.

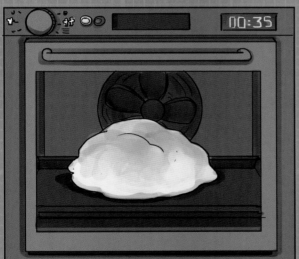

5 Remove the cling film. Preheat the oven to 200°C (400°F or gas mark 6). With an adult's help, put the dough in the oven and bake for 30-35 minutes.

6 Carefully take the baked bread out, and leave to cool. When it's ready, cut a slice and look at the bubbles inside.

WHAT HAS HAPPENED?

Yeast is actually a living thing. It is a type of fungus that is related to mushrooms. When it has water, warmth and a supply of sugar, it starts to feed. As it feeds, it makes bubbles of gas. The bubbles make the dough 'rise' and get bigger.

Mould garden

Mould is a kind of living thing. It is in the fungi family, along with yeast and mushrooms. To see mould growing, grow your own mould garden inside a jar.

You will need:

- Old fruit, old cheese, and stale bread, cake or biscuits
- A cooking knife
- A glass jar with a tight-fitting lid
- Sticky tape
- Water
- Pen and sticky label

1 Chop up your food items into chunks. Sprinkle each one with water, and put them inside the jar.

2 Screw on the lid tightly. Then wrap sticky tape around the edge of the lid too, for an extra-tight seal.

3 Write 'Mould Garden — do not open!' on your sticky label, then stick it onto the jar.

4 Put the jar in a safe place where no one will throw it away or play with it.

5 Check the jar every day. Eventually, you should see mould starting to grow on the food.

6 When you've finished with the experiment, throw the jar away, unopened. Mould can be bad for you — it's best not to let it escape.

Try this!
Try looking more closely at the mould with a magnifying glass. Can you see different types of mould? Can you see little stalks or hair-like parts?

WHAT HAS HAPPENED?

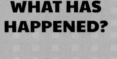

Like mushrooms and toadstools, moulds release tiny spores into the air. The spores work like seeds. If they land on food, they can start to grow into new moulds. As food starts to get old, mould collects and grows on it.

Mould grows hairs, like tiny roots, into the food to feed on it.

Spores

Spinning pictures

You will need:

- Thick card
- Scissors
- Hole punch
- String
- Felt-tip pens

It is easy for your eyes to get confused. If you see things spinning very quickly, they can seem to blend together into one.

1 Cut out a circle of card about 8 centimetres (3 inches) across. Use the hole punch to make a hole on each side.

2 Cut two pieces of string, then thread one through each hole. Tie each string in a knot to hold it in place.

3 In the middle of the card, draw a simple picture, such as a goldfish or a bird. Flip the card over so that it is upside down.

4 Draw another picture on the other side to go with the first picture, such as a goldfish bowl or a bird cage.

5 Hold the strings on either side of the card, close to the holes. Twist your fingers to make the card spin over and over.

Another fun idea

Here are some more ideas for pictures. Can you think of others too?

Did you know?

This experiment was invented over 150 years ago. In the 1800s, it was called the 'thaumatrope'.

WHAT HAS HAPPENED?

Your eyes work by detecting patterns of light, and sending signals to your brain. When you see an image, it lasts for a little while in your brain, even if it has disappeared in real life. The spinning card moves so fast that both images end up in your brain at the same time, and seem to get mixed together.

6 As you watch the card spinning, can you see the two pictures appear as one image?

Grabbing hand

Reach out your hand and pretend to grab something. Your fingers curl up towards each other. How do they do that? Find out with this model hand.

You will need:

- Card
- Pens
- Scissors
- Straws
- Sticky tape
- String

1 Draw around your hand and wrist onto the card. Cut the shape out using the scissors. Colour it in too, if you like!

2 On the card hand, mark each finger into three sections, like real fingers. Fold the fingers between the sections, like this.

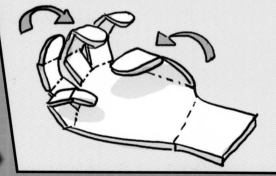

3 Cut pieces of straw slightly shorter than each finger section. Tape the pieces of straw onto the fingers so that they line up.

4

Tape longer pieces of straw onto the palm of the hand, leading from each finger to the wrist. Make sure they all end at the same place.

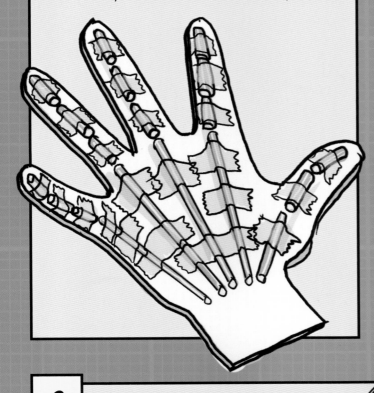

5

Cut five long pieces of string. Thread them through the straws for each finger, and tape them in place at the fingertips.

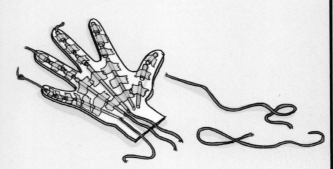

Try this!
Hold your arm tightly, about halfway between your wrist and your elbow, and wiggle your fingers. You should be able to feel the muscles and tendons moving.

6

Now hold the hand by the wrist, and gently pull on the string. Your hand will curl up and grab, just like a real one!

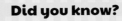

Did you know?
Many animals have body parts that work the same way – like a chicken's foot or a tiger's paw.

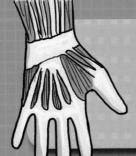

WHAT HAS HAPPENED?

Your body contains muscles that make you move by pulling on your bones. The muscles that move your fingers are in your arms. They are connected to stringy parts called tendons that connect to your fingers.

Blink reflex

A reflex is something your body does by itself, without you deciding to do it. Reflexes can be useful, as they help to protect us.

You will need:

- A door with a glass window in it, or a ground-floor window
- Cotton wool balls
- Two or more people

1 One person should stand behind the glass, with their face up close to it and their eyes wide open.

2 Another person should stand on the other side of the glass, and throw cotton wool balls at the first person's face, one at a time.

3 The first person has to try not to blink. When they've had a go, swap places. It's very hard to keep your eyes open!

Did you know?
Your blink reflex protects your eyes from dangers like flying sand or insects.

WHAT HAS HAPPENED?

Your blink reflex makes your eyes shut if anything moves quickly towards your face. Even though you know the glass is in the way, it's very hard to stop your eyes from shutting.

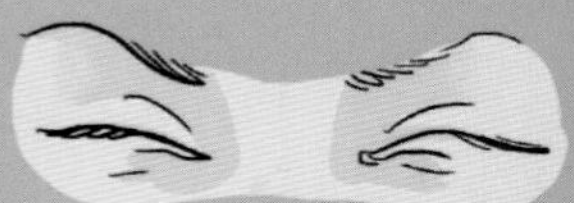

Food tubes

When you eat food, it goes into your stomach, then travels through a long set of tubes called intestines. Let's find out how long they are!

1 First, ask someone to measure how tall you are. Write down the results on your paper.

130 cm (51 inches)

2 Use the calculator to multiply your height by five. Write down the answer on the paper.

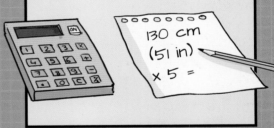

130 cm (51 in) x 5 =

3 The answer shows how long your intestines are! Measure out a piece of string that long.

WHAT HAS HAPPENED?

You have two intestines – the small intestine and the large intestine. The small intestine soaks up food chemicals into your body. Its length is about four times your height. The large intestine collects waste and turns it into poo. It's about the same length as your height.

Your intestines are coiled up in loops and folds. That's how they fit inside you!

95

Glossary

air pressure The force of air as it pushes on things.

centre of gravity The point that marks the centre of an object's weight, so that it acts as a balancing point.

chemical reaction A process where substances undergo a change to form a different substance.

electrons Tiny specks of matter with a negative electrical charge.

evaporates Turns from a liquid into a gas.

friction A force that slows moving objects.

gas A substance that is like air and has no fixed shape.

microorganism A living creature that is too small for us to see with the naked eye, such as a bacterium.

molecules The smallest part of a substance that is still defined as that substance.

refraction The bending of a ray of light as it passes through one substance into another, such as from air into water.

sound wave A vibration that is produced when a sound is made, and is responsible for carrying sounds to the ear.

spore A reproductive cell that grows into a new plant, found on ferns and moulds.

static A form of electricity that is produced by friction.

surface tension A force of resistance felt on the surface of a liquid.

vibrate To move from side to side, or back and forth, very quickly.

Index